THE MINISTRY

OF

EVANGELIZATION

Susan W. Blum

THE LITURGICAL PRESS
Collegeville, Minnesota 56321

Cover design by Ann Blattner. Photo by S. Annette Brophy.

7   8   9

Contents

Preface

Evangelization: A Life-Changing Ministry

All right, I think I have always been hooked on Jesus but was afraid to mention it. Like politics and sex, Jesus was not polite dinner-table conversation.

After becoming a convert to the Catholic Church more than twenty-five years ago, I have had an ever-increasing desire to share my faith with others. It was not until 1979, though, that I "came out of the closet," and my life has not been the same since. From being a rather ordinary Catholic housewife, uninvolved in my parish other than teaching a CCD class, I became a journalist, author, magazine editor, ecclesial lay minister, graduate student, educator, program developer, lecturer, conference speaker, preacher, and beggar for the poor.

In that year the Paulist National Catholic Evangelization Association sponsored its first Lay Celebration of Catholic Evangelization in Washington, D.C. I was intrigued to see Catholic laypeople—ordinary men and women—sharing their faith so strongly, so effectively, so joyfully.

I returned home to Florida from Washington and did three things, all of which turned into life-changing experiences. The first thing I did was write my first newspaper article. I was so excited about what I had seen and heard in Washington that I wanted to share it with the whole world. In my enthusiasm, I wrote a detailed account of the wonderful world of Catholic lay evangelization and submitted it to Gerard Sherry, then editor of Miami's diocesan newspaper, *The Voice.*

I did not know that writers weren't supposed to submit twenty-three-page articles. Mr. Sherry was kind when he offered to publish it in sequels. Three issues later, Miami Catholics, at least, had read about lay evangelization, in both English and Spanish, and my new career in journalism was launched.

Then, I went to see Archbishop Edward A. McCarthy to tell him that the archdiocese needed a good evangelization commission. He smiled.

The third thing I did was to visit my pastor, Rev. Ronald J. Pusak of St. Joan of Arc Church in Boca Raton, Florida, to tell him that our parish needed a good evangelization committee. He smiled, too.

For nearly six months, I bugged them both, writing proposals and propositions which I felt they couldn't refuse. Finally, I received a letter from Archbishop McCarthy saying that he was establishing an Evangelization Council and asking me to serve as one of three lay representatives.

A few days later, my pastor called to ask me to coordinate a parish evangelization committee.

To this day I marvel at the responsiveness of these two men. Archbishop McCarthy did a complete turnabout on evangelization. This is the same man who, four years later, was the *only* bishop to stand on the floor at the National Conference of Catholic Bishops' annual meeting and argue for continued funding for the Ad Hoc Committee on Evangelization.

In the same vein, Father Pusak who had hesitated at first, became one of the strongest proponents of parish-based evangelization. In Dr. Glenn Smith's popular book *Evangelizing Adults*,[1] St. Joan of Arc Parish is the *only* Catholic parish mentioned alongside Robert Schuller's Crystal Cathedral, Oral Roberts' City of Hope, and Billy Graham's Evangelistic Crusades.

My interest in evangelization changed my life and gave it new directions. As a result of my newspaper article, I began free-lance writing for *The Voice* and other Catholic diocesan and national publications. As a result of serving on the Archdiocesan Council where I eventually became the only layperson among three bishops, ten priests, and three or four sisters, I became acutely aware of my lack, as a convert, of theological training and went back to school for the first time in over twenty years. Within a year's time, I completed a master's degree in pastoral ministry.

As coordinator of parish evangelization, I became increasingly aware of the tremendous needs of the people both within and without the parish and of the energy and enthusiasm of the grass-roots evangelizers who served on our committee.

We were a small band of amateur evangelizers who really didn't know what we were doing, but we learned along the way. We did so many interesting, delightful things in evangelization; this was a particularly grace-filled period of my life. We established monthly Communion breakfasts where we invited the inactive and unchurched members of our community to a country club to hear the personal testimonies of our parish members and even celebrities. We started a parish newsletter, the *Goodnewsletter*; we began a "Welcome Home" program for inactive Catholics and a telephone hot line for angry or disenchanted Catholics. We established a "Welcome to Our Parish" program for newcomers.

One of our most significant innovations was a home visitation ministry every Tuesday evening. Because we didn't have any viable Catholic evangelistic tracts or pamphlets to leave in the homes we visited, we decided to found the Catholic Evangelism Press to provide what we needed. Without any publicity or advertising, we began to receive requests from throughout the United States for these tracts and then, eventually, from Central and South America. We translated our tracts into Spanish and have since distributed hundreds of thousands of them throughout the United States, Canada, the Caribbean, Central America, South America, Africa, and Asia.

In 1982, we decided that the world needed a good Catholic evangelistic magazine, so we founded *The Catholic Evangelist* magazine. Since I was the only one in the group with any journalistic background, limited as it was, I became the founding editor.

Before we went to press, we researched the topic of Catholic and secular magazine publishing. Time and again we were told not to contemplate publication unless we had half a million dollars in the bank. We had 783 dollars and a handful of subscribers when we published our first issue. In the four years of its existence, we reached a circulation of over 15,000 subscribers in all fifty states and in more than thirty foreign countries, not bad for amateurs.

I soon found myself in partnership with Chet Stokloza and Bob Deshaies, founders of the Catholic Evangelistic Center in Blackstone, Massachusetts. They had written a training manual for evangelists, *On Becoming an Evangelist*, in 1976 and had developed training institutes for lay evangelists.

In 1982 we joined forces and combined the best of their training program with the best of the training program we had been using in our parish,[2] which included actual on-the-job training in homes. The result of this collaboration was a new training manual, *Mission: Evangelization*, and, eventually, a new spiritual awakening process for parishes which we called *Isaiah 43*, based on the beautiful forty-third chapter of Isaiah in which God reveals once again his unconditional love for each of us.

Isaiah 43 is basically a "new-fashioned" parish mission, to which we have added extensive follow-up programs in both evangelization training and personal spiritual renewal. So, now, instead of just training lay evangelists, we are offering Parish Missions as well. What fun it is now to be able to preach to and teach hundreds of people in the parishes to which we are invited all around the country.

A significant aspect of the Isaiah 43 process was introduced in 1986 when we joined Food for the Poor, Inc., a ministry to the poor in the Caribbean, founded and directed by Ferdinand G. Mahfood.

Ferdinand and I had been friends for more than ten years when those of us at Isaiah 43 realized that the vital component of social justice was missing from our process. We approached Ferdy who had been feeling the same: that the vital component of evangelization was missing from his social ministry. Evangelization and social ministry are two sides of the same coin, so we joined forces to benefit each other's ministries. Food for the Poor now is the sponsoring agency for our ministry, and we, in turn, beg unashamedly for the poor in the Caribbean at the end of each of our parish missions.

I am nearly three-quarters of the way through my doctoral program in Adult Education, and I find myself teaching more and more at universities and seminaries and in various traditional and nontraditional Continuing Education Programs. Teaching is my first love, and my dream includes designing and implementing a curriculum for Catholic Evangelization in a major Catholic university. Our Protestant friends have been offering professional, academic, degree-granting programs in evangelism for decades, and I think our time has come.

Over the years, I have become an evangelist, and in the process, I have been evangelized and changed. My faith has grown in many new directions; my lifestyle has changed; and my vision of Church has been broadened. I have a lot to say about Catholic evangelization, and most of it comes from personal experience, not just from academic and theological sources.

I am no longer a "closet" evangelization junkie but a full-fledged Catholic lay evangelist who is proud to be a Christian, proud to be a Catholic, proud to be an evangelist!

Whether we are veteran evangelizers or novices, one thing is certain: our lives will never be the same. Welcome to the wonderful world of Catholic evangelization!

Notes

1. Glenn Smith, *Evangelizing Adults* (Mahway, N.J.: Paulist Press, 1987).

2. "Good News Outreach Ministry" (Miami: Archdiocese of Miami Office of Evangelization, 1985).

1

Understanding Evangelization

The ancient concept of the ministry of evangelization has been reintroduced and redefined since 1975 when Pope Paul VI wrote his historic and challenging exhortation to the whole Church, *Evangelii Nuntiandi*, "The Gospels Must Be Proclaimed."

With this new emphasis on evangelization has come confusion and innovation. *Evangelization* is not yet a household word for most Catholics, whether clergy or laity. Where there is familiarity with the term, there is often confusion concerning its meaning.

As Catholics, we have always evangelized, but perhaps we have not identified it as such. Where did we first learn of Jesus? Who taught us our first prayers? Who passed on their faith to us? And to whom are we passing on our faith? Over the centuries the Catholic faith has been passed down and preserved. That's evangelization.

However, many Catholics see evangelization as something which Protestants do. The images of tent-rockers and door-knockers come to mind, and Elmer Gantry prevails as the leading Bible-thumping, money-pumping tent evangelist who, at the conclusion of the popular movie of the sixties, based on Sinclair Lewis' novel of the twenties, finally gives in to his more carnal desires.

Add to this image, the scandals of the television evangelists of the late eighties in the Protestant world, and we come up with a negative, distorted view of authentic evangelization.

Many Catholics who do think of evangelization within a Catholic context relate it to missionary sisters and priests who go into the dark recesses of the steamy Amazon or the deepest jungles of Africa to convert thousands of heathen, head-hunting cannibals.

On a less dramatic scale, we view Catholic evangelization here at home as the work of parish priests who welcome inquirers and teach convert classes. The sisters of the parish might become involved, also, but we generally see parochial evangelization as Father's job or as Sister's job.

The good news about Catholic evangelization today is that it is everyone's job. It is not a Protestant phenomena; it is not oriented toward foreign missions; and it is not limited to the local clergy and religious. Evangelization is the role of *all* believers, and it is precisely in this newly defined role that many Catholics find both challenge and frustration.

In the opening paragraphs of his exhortation to the whole Church on evangelization, Pope Paul VI writes:

> May these words succeed to give a fresh impulse to everyone, the whole People of God assembled in the Church, so that each one of them may follow 'a straight course in the message of the truth,' and may work as a preacher of the Gospel and acquit himself perfectly of his ministry (EN 5).

Later on, he quotes the Vatican II document *Ad Gentes*, writing, "The whole Church is missionary, and the work of evangelization is a basic duty of the People of God" (EN 59).

If evangelization truly is our basic duty, then perhaps it would be helpful to come to grips with exactly what is expected of us. What is evangelization? Where do we fit in? How do we do it?

Before I define evangelization, let me illustrate what it is *not*. In an old *Peanuts* cartoon, Lucy turns around at school and announces to Charlie Brown, "Do you know that I would make the world's best evangelist?" "What makes you think that, Lucy?," he replies. "Would you stand on street corners and preach?" "No," she answers. "Well, would you quote the Bible all the time?" Again, she replies negatively. "Well, what makes you think you'd be the world's best evangelist then?" "It's simple," the curly-haired little girl responds; "I'd just pick up my lunch box and hit them over the head with it!" This is *not* what Catholic evangelization is all about. We are not out to hit people over the heads with anything. Instead, evangelization is a process, a very gentle process.

Evangelization Defined

The official definition of evangelization comes from Pope Paul's document *Evangelii Nuntiandi:*

> For the Church, evangelizing means bringing the Good News into all the strata of humanity, and through its influence transforming humanity from within and making it new. . . .
>
> The purpose of evangelization is therefore precisely this interior change, and if it had to be expressed in one sentence the best way of stating it would be to say that the Church evangelizes when she seeks to convert, solely through the divine power of the message she proclaims, both the personal and collective consciences of people, the activities in which they engage, and the lives and concrete milieu which are theirs (EN 18).

Quite a mouthful, eh? Evangelization can become a complex and complicated issue, and it is this complexity which currently causes confusion and even disagreement among the leadership in the Church and among the leadership of the evangelization movement itself. Over the years, I have observed five different styles of evangelization, none of which, I believe, is complete in itself.

Incomplete Approaches

Some say that evangelization only means inviting people into membership in the Roman Catholic Church; I call this the *affiliative* approach to evangelization. For these people, effective evangelization occurs when new members join the Church or when inactive members return. The criterion for success is based on the fact that new or lapsed members are now officially on the roster and have been incorporated into the Body of Christ, the Church.

Other evangelizers say that the only determiner of effective evangelization is that the person evangelized has accepted the invitation to receive Jesus into his or her heart in a personal relationship. I call this second approach the *foundational* approach. The emphasis here is strictly on the individual's personal, private response to Jesus' invitation.

Still others say that *everything* we do in the Church is evangelization, so why do we need an evangelization committee in the parish, or an Evangelization Office in the diocese? The liturgists say that they are evangelizing; the religious educators say that they are evangelizing. I call this third attitude the *specialization* approach; in it, evangelization is compartmentalized and creates competition and confusion rather than collaboration and unity among the various ministries within a parish or diocese. Each separate ministry—whether it be liturgy, catechesis, social justice, youth, or any other ministry— views itself as an evangelizing ministry and operates in a vacuum without consulting the other ministries or having an overall plan. "Turfism" is the result, and when this occurs, Fr. Patrick Brennan, Founding President of the National Council for Catholic Evangelization, says, "We become stuck in a competitive rut of defending our own kingdoms."[1]

A fourth approach, which because it is passive, is not really an approach at all, is the *historical or traditional* approach. Proponents of this non-approach method say that we have always evangelized, so let's just keep doing what we have been doing. This non-approach to evangelization represents a passive attitude of people uninterested in change or pastors and staff who are tired, overworked, and who view evangelization as just another program or another project in an already overcrowded schedule. Evangelization is not a priority for them, and it is not on their agenda.

Proponents of a fifth approach, the *social action* approach, judge the effectiveness of evangelization by its results: If people are out in the world performing apostolic acts of charity and justice, they must already be evangelized. This approach assumes conversion *(metanoia)*, and the evangelized would include right-to-lifers, soup-kitchen workers, anti-nuclear activists as well as housewives who welcome their new neighbors with a freshly baked cake or loaf of bread. In other words, if they walk like ducks and talk like ducks and act like ducks, they must be ducks.

While all of these approaches have some merit, they have obvious weaknesses. What we need today is an *integrative* model of evangelization which combines the positive aspects of all five of these approaches. An integrative model would include affiliation, personal relationship with Christ, and continuation of tradition. This model would operate on the diocesan and parish levels where all of the ministries would coordinate their pastoral planning. Finally, this integrative model would result in social action and commitment.

These approaches are being debated in the Church today by the theologians and professional ministers of evangelization, both clergy and lay, as evangelization continues to be redefined.

Grass-roots Definitions of Evangelization

At the risk of over-simplification, I would like to offer a few simpler definitions of evangelization which I have arrived at as the result of my own experience as a grass-roots evangelizer. They tend to be inclusive rather than exclusive, broader rather than narrower.

One of my favorite definitions, suggested by a colleague, is simply, "Evangelization is loving people into the Kingdom!"

A second possible and more functional definition is, "Evangelization is inviting people into a loving and personal relationship with Jesus Christ, which is then nurtured by a loving and caring Catholic faith community."

Including both an individual and communal responsibility, a third definition is desired from the Christian psychiatrist Dr. Scott Peck, who in his book *The Road Less Traveled* offers a poignant definition of love. Substituting "evangelization" for "love," the definition becomes: "Evangelization is the process of extending oneself in order to nurture the spiritual well-being of another person."

My favorite definition of evangelization, however, is simply this: "One blind beggar showing another blind beggar where the bread is and both of them being healed in the process." This definition includes the twofold necessity of both possessing and sharing the Good News, presumes that the participants agree to work together in a spirit of mutuality and esteem, and results in ongoing conversion for both the evangelizer and the evangelized.

Evangelization as I see it has several ingredients: (1) first and foremost, *love*—love of God, love of others, love of self; (2) *invitation* into a personal relationship with Jesus; (3) ongoing *conversion*; (4) conscious, active *extension* of ourselves and our communities; (5) the nurture of spiritual growth within the context of a worshipping faith community, and (6) the ministry of loving service to others.

If evangelization has these six vital characteristics, then there are four requirements for effective evangelization:

1) proclamation
2) conversion
3) incorporation
4) service

Pope Paul VI, in *Evangelii Nuntiandi*, has this to say about each of them:

Proclamation: "The Gospel must be proclaimed by witness of lifestyle . . . which includes presence, sharing solidarity . . . the wordless witness of a Christian life" (EN 21).

"Nevertheless, this always remains insufficient. . . . The witness of life sooner or later must be proclaimed by the word of life. There is no true evangelization if the name, the teaching, the life, the promises, the kingdom and the mystery of Jesus of Nazareth, the Son of God are not proclaimed" (EN 22).

Conversion: "But above all, each individual gains this kingdom and this salvation through a total interior renewal which the Gospel calls *metanoia*; it is a radical conversion, a profound change of mind and heart" (EN 10).

Incorporation: "In fact the proclamation only reaches full development when it is listened to, accepted and assimilated, and when it arouses a genuine adherence in the one who has thus received it. . . . Such an adherence, which cannot remain abstract and unincarnated, reveals itself concretely by a visible entry into a community of believers. . . . Thus those whose life has been transformed enter a community which is itself a sign of transformation, a sign of newness of life: it is the Church, the visible sacrament of salvation" (EN 23).

Service: "How in fact can one proclaim the new commandment without promoting in justice and in peace the true, authentic advancement of man? We ourself have taken care to point this out, by recalling that it is impossible to accept 'that in evangelization one could or should ignore the importance of the problems . . . concerning justice, liberation, development and peace in the world. This would be to forget the lesson which comes to us from the Gospel concerning love of our neighbor who is suffering and in need' " (EN 31).

Notes

1. Patrick Brennan, *Catholic Evangelization Today* (Mahway, N.J.: Paulist Press, 1987), p. 192.

2

Role of the Laity as Evangelizers

Whatever our definition is, there is one certainty concerning evangelization that we must always keep in mind: *Evangelization is not an option!*

> The presentation of the Gospel message is *not an optional contribution* for the Church. It is the duty incumbent upon her by the command of the Lord Jesus, so that people can believe and be saved. This message is indeed *necessary*. It is *unique*. It *cannot be replaced.* It does not permit either indifference, syncretism or accommodation. It is *a question of people's salvation.* . . . It merits having the apostle consecrate to it all his time and all his energies, and to sacrifice for it, if necessary, his own life (EN 5—emphasis mine.)

As we continue our discussion of understanding contemporary Catholic evangelization, the role of the laity becomes critical. Ministry, itself, is the issue.

Creative Tension

"Ministry is a New Testament word that in the course of Roman Catholic history became coextensive with priesthood. Today it is having a rebirth," writes Dennis Geaney in his book *Full Church, Empty Rectory.*[1]

Many laypeople and clergy, as well, simply do not acknowledge the authenticity or responsibility of lay ministry today. The concept of the ministry of the laity must be understood and accepted if Catholic evangelization is to continue. From a practical point of view, if Catholic evangelization was once viewed as the role of the ordained or those under vows, it is not so today. There simply aren't enough priests or sisters to go around. With the current and predicted future shortages of religious vocations, the laity must assume their right and responsibility as ministers.

However, the ministry of the laity is not based on the lack of ordained ministers or vowed religious but on the theological principle of the laity's right and responsibility to minister by virtue of baptism.

Richard McBrien succinctly contrasts two extreme views of ministry—that it is restricted to the ordained or that everyone is regarded as called to ministry by baptism: "The first extreme is outdated," he writes in *Catholicism*, "the second not yet fully challenged."[2]

Prior to Vatican II, the laity primarily assumed a passive role. Now, however, the emergence of an active laity, based on many of the documents of Vatican II, has projected a crisis in ministry. It is this struggle of adaptation to a new view of ministry during a transitional age which frustrates both clergy and laity alike.

A creative tension has developed, quite often expressed by Catholic lay evangelists who are frustrated in their role by pastors who neither understand nor accept the ministry of the laity in the Church today. This same tension is voiced by clergy who feel that the laity are somehow deficient, either in their knowledge of Church teaching or their ability to articulate that teaching accurately. Both sides in this constructive conflict have merit.

We now need a truce. Shared ministry must occur for evangelization to be effective, for evangelization is a collaboration in which both clergy and laity respect each others' gifts.

Mutual Responsibility

Both clergy and laity must assume responsibility for a harmonious shared ministry. This call for shared ministry is well stated in the Vatican II document, *Ad Gentes:*

> The Church has not been truly established, and is not yet fully alive, nor is it a perfect sign of Christ among men, unless there exists a laity worthy of the name working alongside the hierarchy. For the gospel cannot be deeply imprinted on the talents, life and work of any people without the active presence of lay people. Therefore, . . . the greatest attention is to be paid to raising up a mature Christian laity (*Ad Gentes*, 21).

While discussing this tension or creative conflict in the context of contemporary Catholic evangelization, we must clearly understand from the beginning that these controversies are not universal in nature. Not *all* Catholic priests resist the laity in their role as evangelizers; not *all* lay evangelizers go unsupported in their role. However, these real or imagined conflicts exist often enough and are reported often enough to merit discussion.

In proposing a national agenda for Catholic evangelization, Marsha Whelan, the second president of the National Council for Catholic Evangelization, stresses the need for "the clear, concrete articulation of the different tasks and roles involved in the evangelization process. This articulation needs to emphasize that professional ordained and non-ordained ministers, as well as lay volunteers who minister within the ecclesial community, share the task of building up the community of believers. . . . Above all, this articulation needs to emphasize and affirm the role of the laity being sent 'into the world'—workplace, neighborhood, family. . . ."[4]

The late Archbishop Dermott Ryan, then pro-Prefect of the Congregation of the Propagation of Faith spoke shortly before his death on this very issue. "In this modern world and in many fields of lay activity, it is often not enough for lay people to be committed. They need to be well informed about their faith and about those aspects of Catholic teaching which relate to their chosen field of activity. Being informed and committed, they must also be able to articulate through the written or the spoken word or the appropriate witness of action, the plan of God for mankind. To be committed and informed without being articulate will blunt the Christian contribution to many fields of activity and reduce the impact in a world which is increasingly dominated by the media. Regretfully, one has to add that many who are articulate are not necessarily well informed and, as a result, represent a form of commitment to the Church which is less than adequate."[5]

Responsibility for resolving this creative conflict concerning the ministry of the laity is twofold: the hierarchy and clergy must affirm and welcome lay ministers, and lay ministers must accept the responsibility of becoming informed and articulate as well as committed to service. This is where, I believe, the tremendous need for training of lay evangelizers arises. A recent survey in the *Notre Dame Study of Catholic Life since Vatican II* indicates that while over fifty percent of Catholics agree that one should share one's faith, only two percent are actually doing so.[6]

Permission, Protection, and Power

Three necessary ingredients, I believe, for effective shared ministry in evangelization are permission, protection, and empowerment.

Scripture itself, as well as the Vatican II documents and *Evangelii Nuntiandi*, give laypeople and clergy alike permission to evangelize. Pope Paul VI defines workers of evangelization:

> This includes ourself as Pastor of the universal Church, our brother bishops . . . priests and deacons. . . . (EN 68).

Religious . . . find in their consecrated life a privileged means of effective evangelization (EN 69).

Lay people . . . must exercise a very special form of evangelization (EN 70).

We receive protection from our belief that evangelization is not an individual, but an ecclesial, act. Pope Paul VI says, "Evangelization is for no one an individual and isolated act; it is one that is deeply ecclesial . . . in union with the mission of the Church" (EN 60).

Empowerment comes from the Holy Spirit, Pope Paul says:

Evangelization will never be possible without the action of the Holy Spirit. . . . the Holy Spirit is the principal agent of evangelization: it is He who impels each individual to proclaim the Gospel, and it is He who in the depths of consciences causes the word of salvation to be accepted and understood (EN 75).

We said in the very beginning that evangelization can be complex. However, if we realize that, first, it is not an option for us; second, that evangelizing is our right and responsibility requiring training; and third, that we are permitted, protected and empowered as lay ministers of evangelization, then we can go on and, as St. Paul writes to Timothy, "fulfill our ministry of evangelization."

Notes

1. Dennis Geaney, *Full Church, Empty Rectory* (Notre Dame: Fides: Claretian, 1980), p. 26.

2. Richard McBrien, *Catholicism*, Vol. II (Minneapolis: Winston Press, 1980), p. 842.

3. Walter M. Abbott, S.J., ed., *The Documents of Vatican II*, "The Decree on the Church's Missionary Activity *(Ad Gentes)*, No. 21 (Chicago: Association Press/Follett Publishing Company, 1966), pp. 610–611.

4. Marsha Whelan, "A National Agenda for Catholic Evangelization," *Catholic Evangelization in America*, (Washington: Paulist National Catholic Evangelization Association, March/April, 1988), p. 48.

5. Dermot J. Ryan, D.D., "Evangelization Ten Years Later—A Look at the Church's Response to the International Synod in Evangelization," *Renewal in Catholic Evangelization* (Gainesville, Florida: Koch Foundation, 1986), pp. 15–16.

6. Joseph Gremillion, James Castillo, *The Emerging Parish: The Notre Dame Study of Catholic Life Since Vatican II* (New York: Harper and Row, 1987).

3

The Recipients of Evangelization

Evangelization is a person-centered ministry, and its core is the person of Jesus Christ. The message of evangelization always remains the same and is centered on Christ. But there are other important people involved in the process of evangelization—the evangelizer and the recipient of evangelization. Let us begin by looking at those whom we are evangelizing.

Sometimes, in the process of developing any ministry—whether it is evangelization, youth ministry, or ministry to the separated and divorced, we tend to group everyone in our particular ministry together and generalize in terms of the results of the most recent sociological or psychological studies. We must always keep in mind that each of the inactive Catholics or each young person or each separated or divorced person is exactly that—a person. Each person is unique and has different needs.

Evangelization is a *personal* ministry, and we need to develop a keen awareness of the individuality of each person we approach. So, we ask ourselves, "Whom are we called to evangelize?"

Evangelization surveys generally divide the population of the United States into five main groups, four of which we are called to evangelize:[1]

Fifty-two million active Catholics—defined as attending Mass at least four times a year.

Fifteen million inactive Catholics—defined as attending Mass fewer than four times a year, most not attending at all, except possibly Christmas and Easter.

Eighty million unchurched Americans, about forty-one percent of the total population of the United States.

Twelve million non-Christian religious—six million of whom are members of the Jewish faith.

Seventy-five million non-Catholic Christians—We are not attempting to evangelize (proselytize) this group. We are not into "pew-snatching!"

Evangelizing Active Catholics

"Why on earth should we be concerned with evangelizing our own members, people who are actively involved and attend Mass?" you might ask. Remembering that evangelization is an on-going process, we offer several reasons.

First, we can only share with others what we know ourselves. If our own faith is not strong or if we do not really believe the "good news," how can we share it with others? "The Church is an evangelizer, but she begins by being evangelized herself" (EN 15).

In 1984, George Gallup, Jr. completed an interesting study of all Christian denominations, including Catholicism, and he shared the results in a one-hundred-page report entitled "Religion in America." In this report, Gallup finds that only twelve percent of the population is among the "highly spiritually committed" and that these people are "a breed apart from the rest of the populace."[2]

He goes on to say that "very little difference is found in the behavior of the churched and the unchurched on a wide range of moral and ethical items. . . . However, dramatic differences were found in the behavior of the "highly spiritually committed" compared with those of the less spiritually committed, with the "committed" showing a much higher level of moral conduct.

"The highly committed," Gallup continues, "are

1) more satisfied with their lot in life;

2) far happier than others;

3) place greater importance on family life;

4) more tolerant of other races and religions;

5) are vitally concerned about the betterment of society; and

6) are far more involved in charitable activities than are their counterparts.

"The majority of church people, those less committed," he states, "fall into 'the category of nominal Christians,' and their ethical behavior is little different from the unchurched."

Based on the results of this study, the challenge clearly exists, both within and without the Church, to strengthen the religious commitment of both the churched and the unchurched.

Another reason exists for evangelizing active Catholics. It has been widely accepted that Catholics are over-catechized and over-sacramentalized but under-evangelized. We tend to assume conversion *(metanoia)* has already occurred.

Granted, there are many types of conversion, but what I refer to here is the conversion, the *metanoia,* of which Pope Paul VI speaks: "the total interior renewal, a radical conversion, a profound change of mind and heart" (EN 10).

At the same time, I go back to the original premise that evangelization is a process of continual and progressive conversion. In other words, none of us have arrived. Through evangelization, we ourselves are constantly being converted.

The means of evangelizing active Catholics vary, but an all-parish revival is often necessary since renewal which is restricted to small, isolated groups often becomes divisive.

Several popular programs of renewal are available such as Renew, Parish Renewal, Christ Renews His Church, and other lesser known programs, including the Isaiah 43 Spiritual Awakening Process.[3] A renewed parish becomes itself an evangelizing parish reaching out and welcoming strangers.

Evangelizing Inactive Catholics

In the United States today there are an estimated fifteen million inactive Catholics, averaging about 800 per parish. It is estimated that one out of four baptized Catholics is now inactive.[4]

In his book *Why Catholics Leave*, Rev. Glenn Smith suggests the following reasons why, according to a Gallup poll, they leave the Church.[5]

1. Marriage to a non-Catholic spouse—this number continues to grow, now affecting one out of every three marriages. Statistics indicate that approximately fifty percent of all those who marry non-Catholic spouses will eventually stop practicing their Catholic faith.

2. The ineffective preaching of the clergy—social issues do not interest the average American Catholic, who looks for a presentation and application of the Word of God and for spiritual answers to life's basic problems and questions, not for duties and social obligations.

3. The low state of music and liturgical celebrations—according to a Gallup poll, as many Catholics left because of too little change as have left because of too much liturgical change.

4. A personal or family quarrel with a priest, sister, brother, parish community—or a real or fancied insult or act of rejection by a religious leader.

5. The impersonalism of the large Catholic parish—"The Church isn't really interested in me, whether I stay or leave." In America, the average Catholic parish has over 2,500 people, while the average Protestant church has fewer than two hundred members.

6. Conflict over artificial birth control, remarriage after divorce, and the ordination of women.

7. Mounting crisis of authority—growing differences in what the ordinary Catholic thinks and does and what the Pope

and the bishops teach. The widening split between what the theologians say and what the bishops teach.

8. The "cool" life—which is in conflict with what the Church teaches.

9. Mobility—"I got out of the habit of going." Twenty percent of our population moves every year; the single most common reason for stopping church attendance is a physical move from one place to another, and with no spiritual roots, people simply drift away. Also, for many, vacation times and recreational programs have affected their Sunday worship, until the regularity of attendance is broken.

The same Gallup poll reports the five major answers to the question asked of teenagers, "Why is the Church failing?":

1. Churches are not reaching out to the people they ought to be serving.

2. Churchgoers and church members have too many negative attitudes.

3. Churches are failing to deal with the basics of faith and are not appealing to youth on a deeper spiritual level.

4. There is little feeling of excitement and warmth in churches.

5. There is a low opinion of the clergy.

Evangelizers might be tempted to look down upon inactive Catholics or misinterpret their reasons for leaving as excuses or rationalizations. However, it is important for us to accept these people where they are. For one reason or another, they have made the decision not to participate in the Roman Catholic Church. They are adults, and we must listen to them, acknowledge them, and invite them in a spirit of reconciliation to come home.

We must be very careful that we are not judgmental or non-accepting of the inactive Catholics among us who very well might be our own parents, spouses, children, friends, or neighbors. I know that some twenty years ago, my family left the Church, and I frequently felt a strong sense of superiority from those friends and relatives who were active Catholics. I felt that we were being judged harshly and unfavorably.

This period of seeming inactivity in my life was actually a time of spiritual growth for me. I certainly didn't throw out my morality or become a bad person; in fact, I found myself praying more, returning to Scripture, and growing and deepening in faith.

One thing that hurt me very much during this experience was the fact that, even though I had been active and visible in ministry in my parish, no one seemed to notice when I left. How I yearned for someone to call or visit. I was struggling with the institutional Church, and I would have loved to have had some help on the matter. I realize that I could have approached the pastor or one of the associates or someone else in parish leadership; I could have taken the initiative. But I guess that like many other inactive Catholics, I was too angry and too hurt. I would have welcomed, however, someone who, in a loving and caring manner, was sincerely concerned about us.

Our return to the Church occurred about four years later when we moved to a new city and a new parish. Interestingly, the person who facilitated our return was a layman, who warmly invited us "because the parish *needed* us."

Dr. Dean Hoge, a sociologist at The Catholic University of America, has written a fine study of the re-entry of inactive Catholics into the Church. I have kidded him, that his book, *Converts Drop-outs and Returnees*,[6] was named just for me.

Inactive Catholics are often looking for someone to listen to their story and perhaps, in some cases, do something about their situation. Above all, they want to be loved, accepted, needed, and then welcomed back into the Church.

Evangelizing the Unchurched Population

There is a tremendous need for sensitivity and compassion when we deal with the unchurched American. There are eighty million people who fall into this category in the United States, and in the 1978 Gallup study, "The Unchurched American," half of them stated that they were willing to belong to a church, if invited.[7]

Who are the unchurched?

1. "Baptized pagans" who received no church education or church-going experience after baptism.

2. "Force-fed Christians" who, as children, had to go to church, often without their parents, and who gave it up as soon as possible.

3. Unwelcomed Christians who stay at home because they don't feel part of the community. They may be members of television's electronic church.

4. The mobile unchurched, who moved about a good deal and never settled into a church.

5. The alienated who are angry with God or with the Church.

6. The faith-filled, who believe in God, read the Bible and pray as much or more than those attending Church. They simply do not want to participate in organized religion.

7. The indifferent, who see the Church as irrelevant in the twentieth century.

In his address, "Evangelizing the Unchurched," which was part of the nationally televised Pentecost '87, George Gallup, Jr., cited two major trends arising among Americans: the need to belong and the need to find meaning and value in life in general and in their own lives in particular.

When previously unchurched people finally join a church, they join because of their own affiliative needs or the need to make sense out of their own lives, not primarily because of the church's theology.

Personal Ministry

In all of these cases—evangelizing active Catholics, inactive Catholics, or the unchurched—we must constantly remember that while sociological studies have been done on these large groups of people, each individual is unique and has different hopes, dreams, gifts, and needs.

Evangelization truly is a *personal* ministry. Pope Paul VI writes, "The work of evangelization presupposes in the evangelizer an ever increasing love for those whom the individual is evangelizing" (EN 79).

Notes

1. Alvin A. Illig, CSP, "Getting A Handle on Catholic Evangelization" (Washington: Paulist National Catholic Evangelization Association, 1979.)

2. George Gallup, *Religion in America*, The Gallup Report No. 222 (Princeton, N.J.: Princeton Religion Research Center, Inc., 1984), pp. 18–19.

3. Sources for parish renewal:

RENEW: National Office of Renew
        1232 George Street
        Plainfield, N.J. 07062

CHRIST RENEWS HIS PARISH:
        Christian Life Services
        P.O. Box 19192
        Cleveland, Ohio 44119

PARISH RENEWAL: Rev. Charles A. Gallagher, S.J.
        Pastoral & Matrimonial Center
        67 Prince Street
        Elizabeth, N.J. 07208

ISAIAH 43: Susan W. Blum, Coordinator
        Food for the Poor, Inc.
        1301 W. Copans Road
        Pompano Beach, Florida 33064

4. Alvin A. Illig, "Evangelization Approaches," *Renewal in Catholic Evangelization* (Gainesville, Florida: Koch Foundation, 1986), p. 75.

5. Glenn Smith, *Why Catholics Leave*, cited by Illig, "Getting a Handle on Catholic Evangelization," op. cit.

6. Dean Hoge, *Converts, Dropouts and Returnees*, (Mahway, N.J.: Paulist Press, 1984.)

7. George Gallup, *The Unchurched American* (Princeton, N.J.: The Gallup Organization, 1978).

4

Qualities of an Effective Evangelizer

We need to remember that each evangelizer is unique, bringing different gifts and talents to each situation.

From having trained and worked with thousands of effective evangelizers since 1979, I believe that there are specific qualities we can identify which distinguish the effective evangelizer from the sincere, well-meaning, but ineffective evangelizer. Faith is the first and absolutely necessary quality. Joy, enthusiasm, and courage—which I call secondary qualities—naturally flow from it. A third group of characteristics—a basic knowledge of theology, Scripture, moral teachings and communication skills—are helpful skills which can be learned. However, to be effective evangelizers, we do not need to be professional theologians or Scripture scholars. The greatest asset that we bring to evangelization is the ability to be ourselves.

Personal, Intimate, Reciprocal Love of God

Loving God, manifested through His Son, Jesus Christ, is an *absolute necessity* if we are to be effective evangelizers. The evangelizer's love relationship with God is the one requirement for effective evangelization which is absolutely necessary.

I used to think that love of God implied my active, constant love for him, initiated, controlled, and directed toward him by me. Of course, I always felt frustrated that I fell short of loving him as I should. There were times in my life when

I couldn't love him the way I thought he expected me to. I was simply inadequate.

Over the years, I have found that the love of God is actually a two-way street. Not only was I to "love God with my whole heart, my whole strength, my whole mind, my whole soul," but he also loved me. Love of God took on a new meaning that implied reciprocity. It meant his love for me, not just my love for him.

Last year, my daughter Tammy gave me a card for Mother's Day which said on the front "To Mom. I love you so much." Inside, I read, "but the best part is, *I Know You Love Me Back!!!*"

Without the awareness that God loves me back, I was incomplete as an evangelizer and as a Christian. Psychologists tell us that unreciprocated love is the most painful emotional experience that a person can have. So a first and primary requirement for effective evangelization is that we share in a reciprocal love affair with God. Unfortunately, many people today, many Christians, find themselves in exactly this predicament—unreciprocated love—with God.

Unconditional Love

For many, God's unconditional love for them, which they have heard preached about over and over since childhood, simply is not a reality in their lives. Because of their own poor self-esteem, they cannot comprehend a God who loves them as they are, a God who loves them—not in spite of themselves, but because of themselves, because of who they are. They find it difficult to believe that nothing they say or do can ever stop God from loving them.

As parents, we love our children unconditionally. Of course, we may find that it is easier to love them when they are bringing home straight A's on their report cards or when they have just been elected class president. However, do we stop loving a son who announces that he is failing Spanish, a daughter who has fallen in love with someone whom we consider less than desirable, or the child whom we find out has been experimenting with drugs? Of course not.

I have told my four children time and time again that nothing they can say or do will ever stop me from loving them. I may not always appreciate their behavior or condone their activities, but nothing can prevent me from loving them. God loves us unconditionally, also. Nothing that we can say or do will ever stop God from loving us!

David

One of the most beautiful examples of a parent's unconditional love for a child occurred when I was presenting a parish mission in the South. I had been asked to visit an AIDS patient, a handsome young twenty-seven year old. When I first met David, he asked me not to pray for healing for him, for he had already made peace with his God and looked forward to "walking hand in hand with Jesus." He asked me, though, to pray that he would have a peaceful death. Apparently, AIDS patients often suffer horribly painful deaths.

Normally weighing about 185 pounds, David was down to about 120 pounds; his wrists were like toothpicks, his ankles worse as he lay in the hospital bed. He shared some of his story with me.

When he first became ill, he admitted himself to a charity hospital in New Orleans. There were about one hundred other AIDS patients there, all young men in varying stages of dying. As their conditions worsened, he watched them gather all their courage to call their parents to ask if they could come home to die. Usually, these young men had two messages to give their parents: first, that they were gay, for most of the parents were not aware of their orientation; and, second, that they were dying of AIDS.

In every single case, their parents rejected them saying, "As far as I'm concerned, you're no longer my son!" or "Don't ever call again; you're dead already as far as we're concerned!" Three of David's friends died without anyone claiming their bodies.

Eventually, as he became worse, David came to the point where he wanted to call his own parents but was afraid that he, too, would be rejected. Finally, in desperation he dialed his parents in Baton Rouge, his hometown. His mother's immediate response was, "David, I'm coming down to bring you home."

Because of the severity of his illness, David was admitted to a private hospital where, in a private room, he was given the best medical attention possible, surrounded by family and friends.

"You know, Sue," David told me that day, "God must be a lot like my mom. She loves me just as I am!"

I was evangelized that day and even more so when I spoke with David's mother Billie several months after his death. Often, in the final weeks of his illness, Billie climbed into David's hospital bed, wrapping her arms around him. "Sometimes we'd talk; sometimes we'd tell jokes and laugh; sometimes we'd cry; sometimes we'd just share the silence." One sunny Sunday afternoon, Billie climbed into bed with David; he laid his head on her shoulder, and she wrapped her arm around him. David fell asleep, not to awaken again. "He just stopped breathing," Billie reported. I breathed a prayer of gratitude; my prayers had been answered.

The picture of Billie cradling her dying son in her arms has stayed with me as a beautiful image of God, cradling each of us in his arms. Yes, I think David was right; his mother is a lot like God.

And in her grief, she is evangelizing. She has become surrogate mother to several abandoned AIDS patients, she counsels other parents or family members, and she was instrumental in establishing a *refuge* home for abandoned AIDS patients in

Baton Rouge. Billie shares her faith in a God who loves her unconditionally with all whom she encounters. A devout Catholic, she is the first one to admit that she doesn't have all the answers, but she shares her faith in the Resurrected Lord freely—one blind beggar showing the other blind beggars where the bread is.

"Nemo dat quod non habet"

Many Christians, try as they may, cannot own the fact that God called them by name, created them, redeemed them. They cannot believe that they are God's beloved, his delight, the apple of his eye. They do not accept the fact that nothing will separate them from the love of Christ.

They cannot believe that God loves each of us so much that Jesus came into the world—not to condemn the world but to save it. This is incomprehensible to many people today.

While they may believe—or truly want to believe—the historical facts concerning Jesus of Nazareth who was born in a stable, walked the earth, healed people, died on a cross, and rose from the dead, they find it difficult, if not impossible, to understand that Jesus is still with us today, active and alive in our lives, through the power of the Holy Spirit. He said, "I will not leave you orphans. . . . I am sending you a helper, a paraclete (an advocate) . . . and he will help you and guide you and direct you and teach you everything you need to know . . . and empower you!"

Unless an evangelizer is absolutely convinced of the reciprocal love of God, is involved personally with Jesus as friend, confidante, lover, and is consciously aware of the power of the Holy Spirit in his or her life, effective evangelization will not occur.

The old Latin saying, "Nemo dat quod non habet," holds true in the case of Catholic evangelization: we can not give away something which we don't possess.

But once our faith is secure, internalized and owned—even with the doubts and questions we may have from time to time—nothing can stop the process of our own evangelization. Our faith and commitment will deepen, for we are all in a constant state of faith-development. Conversion never ends. We will be amazed at how we ourselves continue to be evangelized as we evangelize others. Our own faith will grow beyond our wildest dreams as we reach out to others to share the incredible love of God.

In John we read Jesus' words, "Live on in my love . . . and the Father and I will come and dwell within you." How preposterous! How presumptuous to think that God himself will come and make his home in us, lowly creatures that we are. Yet this is exactly what happens as we live in his love and extend it to others. Through his Holy Spirit, God becomes a part of us and dwells within us.

"God with skin on"

I love to tell the story of the Protestant minister whose little five-year-old son woke up one night during a terrible storm.

"Daddy, Daddy," he cried from his bedroom, "I'm so afraid of the lightning and the thunder!"

The minister called back to him, "Son, you know that God loves you and cares for you. He will take care of you. You don't need to be afraid."

And the small boy replied, "Daddy, I know that God loves me and cares for me, but right now, I need a 'God with skin on!'"

As effective evangelizers, that is what we are called to be—"God with skin on"—as we share his incredible love with others, loving them into the kingdom.

I need to point out that *we* do not become God, but *God* becomes part of us. We remain fully human and "do not deem ourselves equal with God but instead empty ourselves" so that he might live and dwell within us. It is true that we are called to "become perfect as the Father is perfect," but we must remember that our striving for perfection is constantly in process.

We also need to celebrate our humanness. It is through our humanness that we become "God with skin on" to other people. It is through our joy, our successes, our accomplishments, through our weakness, our failures, our brokenness, that other people are able to identify with us. If we become "too holy" or "too spiritual," people are turned off, and our goal is sabotaged.

I can think of many people who have been "God with skin on" to me, people who have touched my life and, in that loving encounter, have literally brought God to me in person.

That is the primary role of evangelists: to bring God to other people in person, to introduce them to the person of Jesus, and to invite them into a loving, personal relationship with Him. But I am convinced that this task is impossible to accomplish if prospective evangelizers are not already experiencing this dynamic here-and-now loving relationship with Jesus in their own lives.

It is out of this love relationship with God—this incredible, impossible, intimate, and reciprocal love affair—that the other characteristics of effective evangelists flow.

5

Joy and Enthusiasm in Evangelization

The word, "evangelization," means to announce good news. Once evangelizers are sure that they have good news to share, effective evangelization begins.

As we mentioned before, only when people are convinced of the unconditional, reciprocal love of God can they begin to share it with others. It is out of this conviction that other necessary qualities naturally flow.

Joy

Evangelization is serious business. Being a Christian is serious business. However, I sometimes fear that we can take ourselves too seriously. When I begin to take myself and my ministry too seriously, I know I am in trouble.

Evangelization should be fun! Some evangelizers present themselves and their faith in such serious terms, usually in monotones projected from "down-in-the-mouth" attitudes, that I ask, "Where is their joy?"

Communications experts tell us that we send and receive both verbal and nonverbal messages. Facial expressions relay fifty-five percent of the real message, tone of voice thirty-eight percent, and actual words seven percent.[1]

How do we express joy? This is a difficult question to answer, but it seems to me that people who are experiencing the joy of Jesus in their lives are people at peace, resilient, able to trust God even during adversity or crisis, quietly and firmly grounded in the providence of God; who know and know that they know God's love.

Joy is different from hilarious fun or a tremendous sense of humor. Joy does not mean being funny, but there is a sense of joy in people who truly enjoy life and enjoy living. They often see humor in the most serious situations. They are optimists and see the half-filled glass of water as half full rather than half empty.

Joy-filled people laugh a lot. They are genuinely glad to see you. They make you feel welcome and important—a key to effective evangelization, which we will discuss in detail later.

They do not take themselves too seriously, although they more than likely are very serious about their ministries and approach them with seriousness.

They are not pious or always coming across as holier-than-thou. They do not see themselves as already perfect, but, rather, as people in process.

They do not preach or moralize, judge or condemn. Instead, they accept other people where they are. They view themselves and others as "pilgrims on the journey," and they welcome the companionship of others, regardless of how far their faith has developed.

Joy-filled people have the uncanny ability to laugh with those who laugh and to weep with those who weep. They exude a quiet joy from within. It is difficult to describe joy in concrete terms; it's more a case of being able to recognize its presence or absence instinctively.

Pope Paul VI addresses the question of joy as a quality of an effective evangelizer:

> Let us preserve the delightful and comforting joy of evangelizing . . . May the world of our time, which is searching, sometimes with anguish, sometimes with hope, be enabled to receive the Good News not from evangelizers who are dejected, dis-

couraged, impatient or anxious, but from ministers of the Gospel whose lives glow with fervor, who have first received the joy of Christ, and who are willing to risk their lives so that the kingdom may be proclaimed . . . (EN 80).

Enthusiasm

Closely connected to the quality of joy is the quality of enthusiasm. Pope Paul VI begs us to be enthusiastic evangelizers:

Let us therefore preserve our fervor of spirit. . . . May it mean for us—as it did for John the Baptist, for Peter and Paul, for the other apostles and for a multitude of splendid evangelizers all through the Church's history—an interior enthusiasm that nobody and nothing can quench (EN 80).

Are we excited and enthusiastic about the good news which we have to share? Are we really animated when we talk about this God of ours? Do we communicate joy, assuredness, conviction, and truth when we discuss our faith?

Sometimes, as a writer and editor, I have fun taking poetic license with the Gospels. It's not that I would ever presume to rewrite them, but as I enter into one of the scenes or one of the characters, my imagination takes over and I end up with a slightly different version.

One of these versions includes a description of Mary Magdalene's excitement after she realized that Jesus was not in the tomb, that he had indeed risen from the dead as he promised.

In Matthew's account, the women see both an angel and Jesus Himself; in Mark's gospel, they see a young man dressed in a white robe; in Luke's gospel, they see two men in dazzling garments; and in John's version, two angels in dazzling robes appear, as well as Jesus himself—initially as a gardener. All the gospel accounts have the same message for the women: He is not here. He has been raised up from the dead. Do not weep. Do not be afraid. Go and tell the others.

Probably one of the most understated passages in Scripture occurs in all four of the Gospels as the evangelists describe Mary Magdalene's response. "Mary Magdalene," according to John 20:18, "went to the disciples. 'I have seen the Lord,' she announced. Then she reported what he had said to her."

My version would read a little differently. Here was a woman who had enjoyed an intimate relationship with Jesus during His lifetime. She was mourning the loss of a good friend, a friend whom she believed to be the Son of God. She was confused and angry.

Then, whether it was one angel, two of them, or Jesus himself who reveals the fact of the resurrection, she is convinced that Jesus lives! If I had been in her situation, I cannot imagine merely "announcing" or "reporting" what I had heard and seen.

My version, and what I think really happened, would probably read more like this:

When she understood that Jesus was alive, had actually risen from the dead, and had appeared to her and the other women, Mary Magdalene hiked up her skirts so she would not stumble and raced all the way back to the Upper Room to tell the others. Running at full speed through the briars and brambles, over rocks, and through streams, she arrived breathless at the door of the Upper Room.

Flushed and excited, eager and anxious to tell the others the good news, she found the door locked and bolted from the inside where the men were all quivering and hiding in fear. She banged and pounded on the door, and finally, when they realized who it was, they opened the door a crack to let her in.

"I have seen the Lord!", she exclaimed excitedly to them. "He is alive! He is not dead! All that He told us is true!" She jumped up and down with joy and danced about the room as she shouted out her message. She hugged each of them as she shared her good news with them about their Lord and friend. She gave them each a slap on the back and a "thumbs up" signal of victory. "Alleluia!," she shouted.

Obviously, I have taken great freedom with Mary Magdalene's response to her encounter with the risen Christ. But I can't imagine her reacting other than with tremendous joy, excitement, and zeal to tell the others.

When I encountered the risen Christ personally, I might have had a feeling of incredulity, of awe at first, but eventually, when I realized that this truly was the living Christ, active and alive in my own life, I couldn't wait to tell my friends all about him!

It is this same excitement which is so necessary for effective evangelization. It flows out of our experience, and most importantly, it is contagious. Someone once said, "Faith is caught not taught!"

We do not need to be constantly slapping people on the back, giving the "thumbs-up" sign and shouting "Alleluia!". There is a time for high-spirited enthusiasm. but there is also a time for what Pope Paul VI calls our "inner enthusiasm."

For effective evangelization to occur, enthusiasm must exist. The word itself means "God within you." If evangelizers are not enthusiastic about sharing the good news in their lives with others, people will know immediately if they try to fake it. Their enthusiasm must be genuine and will be if it comes from an authentic relationship with Christ.

Notes

1. Blum, Deshaies, Stokloza, *Mission: Evangelization* (Boca Raton, Fl.: Catholic Evangelism Press, Inc., 1986), p. 64.

6

The Courage to Evangelize

At the beginning of each Institute on Evangelization which my colleagues and I present, we ask the participants to list the obstacles to evangelization which they experience.

The word *fear* is always at the top of the list. These committed Catholic Christians who are experiencing the risen Christ alive in their lives and who have a strong desire to share this Savior with others are *afraid* to evangelize.

What are their specific fears? First, they fear rejection. They are terrified that if they say to someone that Jesus Christ is their Lord and Savior, they will be rejected personally. They fear that they will somehow be devalued in the eyes of the person who hears them.

Second, they fear that the hearer will judge them and say, "Who are you, with all your imperfections, to be speaking of God and faith to me?" The trainees think that they have to be perfect before they can evangelize.

They fear being asked questions that they cannot answer. They are afraid that their own knowledge, particularly of current Church teaching and Scripture, is inadequate and that they should be experts before they go out to evangelize.

They fear loneliness and isolation. They are afraid that if they become active evangelizers, their family and friends will abandon them as religious fanatics, Jesus freaks, or kooks.

Our trainees often express their fear of the commitment involved, of the time it will take up in a life already overcommitted.

They often say that they fear their inadequacy. They simply don't know how to evangelize. They have never been taught a method by which they can effectively evangelize, and they don't know where to start.

These fears are valid, and we always acknowledge and listen to them. In fact, we have the participants write their fears down on large sheets of newsprint, and we post them around the room as a constant reminder of what some of the goals of the course are. During our nine-day Institutes or during our missions which offer a day-long Introduction to Evangelization, we address each of their expressed fears which vary from parish to parish and attempt to overcome them.

These fears are real; it takes courage to evangelize. Even though I have evangelized people for a good many years and have taught others how to evangelize, there comes that moment during an encounter with another person when I take a deep breath, utter a quick prayer to the Holy Spirit and then dig in. It still takes courage, and that is what I pray for in any evangelistic encounter.

One of the most experienced home visitors in my parish still says that the longest walk is the walk from the car to the front door. He and his partner still pray all the way, not knowing what they will find on the other side of the door.

Evangelization requires a holy boldness since sometimes evangelizers step in where angels fear to tread. Yet our greatest fear, when we first started our Home Visitation Evangelization Ministry at St. Joan of Arc, was that doors would be slammed in our faces.

After eight years of home visitations, our problem is not getting into the homes; our problem is getting out of them. It is amazing how people open up to us and love to talk about their faith experiences once they realize we are there not only to share our faith but also to listen to theirs. Once we give them permission—we, in essence, say, "Hey, it's okay to talk about your faith experiences." They are most eager to share their own experiences or lack of them or their anger or frustration.

One of our earliest trainees was scared to death to go out on his first home visit. "I feel so inadequate," he moaned. Returning from the visit, he was dancing with joy. "You'll never believe it. They were so receptive. Even though I felt totally inadequate, the Lord just seemed to take over. At one point, I thought that it was a set-up and that you had sent me to someone who had already been trained in this process. They asked all the right questions, which led me right into my presentation of the Gospel and the invitation to receive Christ in a new way." He concluded, very wisely, "Thank God for my feeling of inadequacy. I suppose that if I had gone in there feeling totally in control, I wouldn't have allowed the Holy Spirit room to do his thing. That's who was in control from the minute I rang the doorbell."

Another time, a sister who had taken our nine-day course was ready to go out on her first home visit. She was terrified, and she later confided to me that she had wept and wept out of fear. She, too, returned from her first visit rejoicing. She now is head of evangelization training for her whole diocese.

"Second Holy Communion"

Evangelization takes courage. There's no doubt about it. In June 1987, I flew to Washington, D.C., and as I conversed with the woman sitting next to me on the plane I realized that this was an evangelistic opportunity. (More and more, I have come to realize that *every* encounter is an evangelistic opportunity!) I started to feel the butterflies in my stomach, whispered a silent prayer for courage, and thought to myself, "Here we go again!"

The woman in the seat next to me told me that she was going to the wedding of her best friend's son and that it would be the first time in years that she had been in a Catholic Church. "In fact," she said, "the roof will probably fall in!" This is a common remark from inactive Catholics, by the way.

She said that she had been raised Catholic but had been divorced about ten years ago. Since her neighbor told her that she was automatically excommunicated when she divorced her husband, she never went to Mass again. She shared, with tears in her eyes, that she always loved the Eucharist and had a special devotion to Jesus in this Sacrament. "But," she said, "I just can't imagine going to Mass and not receiving Communion. It would be like going to a dinner party and not being included at the dinner table while everyone else enjoyed their meal."

She had not remarried, and I asked her if she was aware that there were no restrictions against her receiving the Eucharist. Again, her eyes filled with tears, and she said, "Do you mean that I could actually receive Communion tomorrow at the wedding? Wouldn't God be awfully mad at me for not going to Mass for all these years?"

"The God that I know would understand your reasons," I replied. "He is a loving God, not a God who came into the world to condemn you." Knowing that she needed a confessor, I suggested to her, "After the rehearsal tonight, why don't you go to the priest and tell him exactly what you have told me. I am *sure* that he will advise you to receive Communion in the morning at the wedding."

As we parted in Dulles International Airport, Nancy hugged me, and the tears were really flowing by then. "I will never forget you," she said. "You have opened a whole new world to me."

Then I prayed like crazy that the priest who was performing the wedding ceremony would be as open to her as I expected. He was. Nancy called me about a week later to say that she had received her "First Holy Communion" again! She said that it was an overwhelming experience and that she joined her local parish and began attending Scripture classes in the evenings. The beauty of it is that she has found Jesus again, and I have made a new friend.

Risks

Yes, evangelization requires courage. But when we realize that we need help and we cry out for help, God comes to our assistance, and through the power of the Holy Spirit, we become effective evangelizers. We become able to take risks, and we risk rejection, loneliness, and the reality of being inadequate.

From the pulpit, one of the retired priests who occasionally assists in our parish offered what is almost an algebraic equation which has changed my life and changed my view of risk-taking. "The degree of your security in your relationship with God is in equal and direct proportion to the degree to which you are willing to take risks."

This "equation" has stuck with me for years, and it boils down to "What's the worst that can happen?" This is a question that I often ask myself when I am in a risk-taking situation. The worst that can happen is not rejection, loneliness, isolation, or someone making fun of me or ridiculing me—but death. And what is death except Graduation Day, the Happy Alleluia Day that I welcome.

In the course of my evangelization activities which have taken me throughout the United States and Canada, I have been in life-threatening situations several times—once on the top floor of a hotel which was on fire and once on an airplane which was struck by lightning. During one parish mission session, I was boldly harassed publicly by a woman in the congregation. In another parish, a woman hit me after one of my Mission talks and then left dramatically by stomping up the center aisle of a standing-room-only church. I have been ridiculed, resented, rejected, and have even received death threats where the F.B.I. was called in because these threats were coming to my home address through the United States Postal Service. Yes, evangelization takes courage.

But, I counter this question, "What's the worst that can happen?", with the question, "What's the best that can happen?" And there are so many positive possibilities, that I just dig in and go for it!

"Going straight to hell"

Probably my most frightening experience during a home visit occurred when my partner and I visited a macho Italian gentleman, probably in his sixties, with shirt opened, hairy chest exposed, and tons of gold chains around his neck.

He looked at us menacingly as we explained who we were and why we had come to visit. We always explain that we have come just to share our faith, not to ask for money or to take census information. We find it helpful to be open about our purpose because most of the people we visit are curious about our reasons for visiting them.

As we began to befriend this man, his wife, and his two married daughters who were present, he remained quiet—not hostile—listening to the conversation. Suddenly, he pounded his fist on the table angrily. "All of this faith talk might be okay for you women, but I know that if I were to die right now, I would go straight to hell! Nobody could ever forgive me for the things I have done in my life," he exclaimed. Avoiding the eyes of his wife and daughters, he shouted, "I have done such awful, terrible things in my life that God would *never* forgive me! In fact, I wouldn't even ask him to forgive me!"

My partner and I looked at each other, frightened and surprised at this violent response. We looked at each other wondering what we should do. This wasn't in the manual!

Our purpose was not to find out what these "terrible, awful" things were, but we assured him—praying all the while—

that Jesus would forgive him if he would give him a chance. "No way!", was the man's adamant response.

Almost simultaneously, we realized what a perfect lead-in his remarks were for our explanation of God's love, compassion and mercy. Talk about Jesus going ahead and preparing the way! "Wow, do we ever have good news for you," we proclaimed.

It took a long time and a great deal of convincing, but the evening ended with this huge, forbidding man on his knees, surrounded by his wife and grown children, praying together with us that Jesus would come into his life in a new and profound way. Tears streamed down the ruddy cheeks of this macho man.

We made an appointment for him to see one of our priests who heard his confession, and now this man and his entire family—wife, children and grandchildren—have all returned to the Church and to the Sacraments. They are active members of the parish, but more importantly, they have returned with a new and stronger relationship with the Lord.

Evangelization takes courage, but it is the Lord who provides that courage, that holy boldness which allows us to go where angels fear to tread.

"Do not fear, little flock, for it has pleased the Father to give you the Kingdom."

7

Celebrating Evangelization

Evangelization is unpredictable, beyond measuring, and addictive. It is a hit-or-miss proposition with absolutely no predictability. Well-planned and executed programs fail; chance encounters bear fruit. Personal invitations fizzle; communal approaches reap the harvest.

Evangelization is a numbers game, not in terms of numbers of converts or of returnees, but as described in Peters and Waterman's popular bestseller *In Search of Excellence.* After observing and interviewing hundreds of corporate executives, they have found that one of the qualities of excellent, high-performing companies is their willingness to play the numbers game in terms of experimentation. Thousands of experiments may have to be made before a few good, solid new products are discovered. In evangelization, hundreds—or perhaps thousands of people—have many different encounters with many different evangelizers before one good, solid conversion occurs. And conversion is the goal of evangelization.

"Perfect Failure"

Evangelization can not be measured. We usually do not know the success or failure of evangelistic efforts. In the excellent, high-performing companies mentioned above, failure is celebrated, as well as success. One of the companies, Heinz's highly successful frozen foods subsidary, Ore-Ida, arranges for a cannon to be shot off to celebrate every time a "perfect failure" occurs. The perfect-failure concept arises from the fact that all research and development is inherently risky and that a good try results in some learning and should be celebrated even when it fails.

We believe that every evangelistic encounter is successful and celebrate each one of them. There is no such thing as an unsuccessful evangelistic encounter. Quite often, our efforts may be dramatically rewarded on the spot with people accepting our invitation to a personal or deeper relationship with Jesus. We are always, however, planting seeds, some of which will die or flourish only for a moment. Only some grow into healthy committed adult Christians. Quite often, we find ourselves watering or fertilizing seeds which someone else has planted. However, whether we are planting, watering, fertilizing, weeding, or reaping the harvest, there is cause for celebration. In evangelization, even apparent failures are to be celebrated; there is no such thing as unsuccessful sowing.

Frustrating and Rewarding

Evangelization is both frustrating and rewarding. The caution here is that we must always remember that the principal agent of evangelization is the Holy Spirit who blows *where* he will, *when* he will.

One aspect of evangelization which can be very frustrating is that we have no sense of control in the process. We are actually powerless when it comes to producing conversion. No matter how hard we try, no matter which methods we choose, no matter how well prepared or how skilled we are, no matter how good our intentions are, it is ultimately the Holy Spirit who will change hearts and minds, not us.

Pope Paul VI recognizes our powerlessness in evangelization:

> Techniques are good, but even the most advanced ones could not replace the gentle action of the Spirit. The most perfect preparation of the evangelizer has no effect without the Holy Spirit. Without the Holy Spirit the most convincing dialectic has no power over the heart of man. Without Him the most highly developed schemas resting on a sociological or psychological basis are quickly seen to be quite valueless (EN 75).

Why Evangelize?

If evangelization is unpredictable, immeasurable, and ineffective by itself, why evangelize? Actually, this is a very good question, one which each evangelizer needs to address. Since the motivation of the evangelizer is a key factor in effective evangelization, it is helpful if we clarify our motives.

The obvious reason for evangelizing is because we are called to be obedient. In Scripture, we are commanded to "Go, therefore, and make disciples of all the world" (Matt 28:19-20). This is the great commission given to us by Jesus after his resurrection.

The Church, also—through doctrine, dogma, and documents—calls us to evangelize, to share our faith. We are reminded that the Church exists to evangelize and that *we* are the Church. It is both our right and responsibility to evangelize.

However, few of us operate from pure obedience, and I have observed other motivations for evangelization. Psychologically, evangelization is addictive because of the infrequent positive reinforcement which we receive from our efforts as evangelizers. Positive reinforcement, which consistently rewards a person's efforts, is a strong motivator of behavior. But unpredictable or intermittent positive reinforcements are even more effective. Regular reinforcement loses its impact when we come to expect it.

Evangelization is not an addiction like chemical dependency in which people have little or no control over their behavior. However, there appears to be a parallel to chemical addiction when infrequent positive reinforcement is a motivator. When an evangelist experiences the joy of evangelizing—usually on an occasional and balanced basis rather than as a predictable and regular "high"—a form of behavioral addiction occurs.

An additional motivating factor, again from the world of psychology, is intrinsic motivation. Neither reinforcement theory nor self-motivation are the starting points for effective evangelization, but they may explain some possible motivations.

Reinforcement theory and self-motivation are basically contradictory to each other, but in the context of evangelization, they are possibly reconcilable. Intrinsic motivation is technical terminology for a simple fact: psychologists have found that people must believe that a task is inherently worthwhile if they really are to be committed to it. They have also found that if a task is rewarded too regularly, the commitment to that task lessens.

This notion of intrinsic motivation is not far fetched at all in the field of spiritual development. Dr. James Fowler addresses it most succinctly. In his book, *Stages of Faith*, he asserts that our master stories—our faith stories, whether implicit or explicit—put into words the values that motivate our lives and the images of power that influence our actions. He states that *we do not put our faith in or commit ourselves to something*—persons, causes, institutions—*because we ought to but because they hold intrinsic worth for us and because they confer value on us.*

So I return to the idea that evangelization is addictive. It gets into our blood and eventually is no longer a program, a process, or even a conscious act; it becomes a way of life. Evangelization becomes ingrained and is as natural as breathing. Every person we meet is enriched and invited by our unconscious evangelistic mindset, demeanor, and lifestyle.

"Compelled to preach"

Finally, I believe that the strongest motivation for evangelization comes from an authentic, internalized owned faith in Jesus Christ through the power of the Holy Spirit. When we have literally fallen in love with Jesus, when we have experienced the good news in our own lives, when we have seen, smelled and tasted the goodness of the Lord, when we have been liberated from darkness into light, from death into life, from tears into dancing, we can not fail to share that life-saving and life-giving message. Like St. Paul, "We are *compelled* to preach the Gospel."

One further thought on the motivation behind evangelization comes from Pope Paul VI, and it is in surprisingly negative terms within a highly positive document that he offers an additional reason for evangelizing:

> It would be useful if every Christian and every evangelizer were to pray about the following thought: men can gain salvation also in other ways, by God's mercy, even though we do not preach the Gospel to them; *but as for us, can we gain salvation if through negligence or fear or shame*—what St. Paul calls 'blushing for the Gospel'—*or as a result of false ideas we fail to preach it?* For that would be to betray the call of God, who wishes the seed to bear fruit through the voice of the ministers of the Gospel; and it will depend on us whether this grows into trees and produces its full fruit" (EN 80, emphasis mine).

My final word on the motivation for evangelization is that it is a lot of fun. The fun comes from new friends we meet, the changes we see in their lives, the joy of sharing the good news in our own lives, and the strong bonds of community and friendship that are formed with other evangelizers. One couple in a Southern parish put it this way, "If you don't evangelize for the love of God or for the love of neighbor, do it for yourself! Do yourself a favor! It really is fun!"

8

Five Steps to Successful Evangelization

There are many different methods of evangelizing, and having had the grass-roots experience of being the coordinator of my parish evangelization committee and a member of our diocesan evangelization council, I have participated in many of these approaches myself. There is no right or wrong way to evangelize. The approaches to evangelizing are only limited by each person's creative imagination. We have, over the years, experimented with mass mailings, communion breakfasts, newsletters, parish surveys, inactive-Catholic groups, welcoming committees, open houses—just about everything short of skywriting. Our theory is if it works, use it.

Over the years, though, I have found that one-on-one encounters seem to be the most effective means of evangelizing in the long run. As a result, my colleagues and I have developed a five-step method which we use to train evangelizers. It must be understood that this is only *one* method of evangelizing, and it is designed specifically for home visitations. Of course, the same method can be adapted for use in any encounter, whether it is a hospital visit or a welcoming visit, whether it is a continuing relationship with a member of your own family or a co-worker, or whether it is a casual encounter with a stranger on a plane. What we have found is that if our trainees can apply these steps within the narrow confines of a limited home visit, they can apply the same method to any encounter.

It is important to realize that we are not saying that home visits are the *only* way to evangelize; we simply offer a viable approach to one way of evangelizing, hoping that people will adapt it to their needs and recognize that many other forms of evangelizing also are effective. If a parish team does not feel that home visitation is appropriate in their community, they may be interested in investigating other means of evangelizing such as welcome-home programs for inactive Catholics or a parish open house to which the whole community is invited. Some parishes and dioceses have found taking a census effective, whereas others have used mass mailings or the media.

We believe that the most effective evangelizing is personal, lay run, and parish centered. This is the method explained in detail in the training manual, *Mission: Evangelization*,[1] in the Evangelization Training Seminars, and Parish Missions. I will try to give an overview of the process here.

Evangelizing a Whole Beauty Parlor

Let me tell you a story first. One day when I was having my hair done, the beautician seated me under a hairdryer next to a woman who was obviously upset. Tears were streaming down her face, so I reached over, took her hand and asked if there was anything I could do to help her.

"No," she tearfully replied. "No one can help me now. Life just isn't worth living." She told me, then, that her husband had died in her arms from a massive heart attack just a few weeks earlier and that she couldn't face living without him. "There's no hope," she cried.

I introduced myself to her and found out that Jean had been raised in the Baptist Church but was not active now in any church. I shared with her that I, too, had once felt the way she did. Although circumstances were different, I had felt that life was not worth living and that I was in a hopeless situation, also. I told her how my faith had strengthened me and was the only consolation that I had at the time.

She was dubious about God even being interested in her. I shared the core message of the Gospel with her, explaining that God certainly was interested in her and, in fact, loved her unconditionally and would come to her assistance if she asked him. Then, I asked if she would like to invite Jesus into her life in a new way, asking him to be her comforter, her consoler in this time of sadness. We held hands and prayed right there under the hairdryer.

Eventually, Jean accepted my invitation to come to Mass with me and later joined the widow and widowers group at church. Two years ago, she asked me to be the matron of honor at her wedding to a terrific man, a member of the singles group. Jean and her husband both have continued ministry formation and Scripture study in our parish and are considering joining our evangelization team.

It is impossible to speak in a normal voice and be heard under a hairdryer, so the whole beauty parlor was evangelized that day! This is an example, however, of how our method can be applied anytime, anyplace.

Five-Step Method

This story illustrates, in a nutshell, our five-step method which includes (1) befriending people, (2) faith sharing, (3) the Christ story, (4) invitation to conversion, and (5) integration into community.

As the following chart illustrates, the process begins and ends with discipleship. To be a disciple means to be a follower of Jesus, to have a deep, dynamic faith in Jesus Christ. Likewise, discipleship is the goal of evangelization. As Pope Paul VI writes, "Finally, the person who has been evangelized goes on to evangelize others. Here lies the test of truth, the touchstone of evangelization: it is unthinkable that people accept the Word and give themselves to the kingdom without becoming people who bear witness to it and proclaim it in turn" (EN 24).

FIVE Steps of Evangelization Process

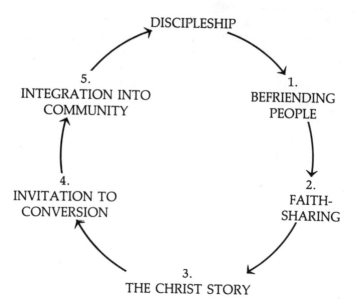

DISCIPLESHIP

5.
INTEGRATION INTO
COMMUNITY

1.
BEFRIENDING
PEOPLE

4.
INVITATION TO
CONVERSION

2.
FAITH-
SHARING

3.
THE CHRIST STORY

Befriending People

The first step in the evangelization process is to befriend people.
Catholic evangelizers never look at people as prospects, as some
other evangelizers do. Our goal is not to convert people to the
Catholic Church but rather—at this stage—to befriend them,
to establish rapport with them in order to proceed to the next
step. We can't just walk into someone's home or life and immediately begin sharing our faith. Common ground, a sense
of identity must first be established.

An evangelizer must have a love and genuine concern for
people, and must receive a certain degree of trust and permission from the person evangelized before continuing with the
process. Also, it is extremely important that evangelizers accept people where they are in a spirit of mutuality and esteem.

Learning to relate to people builds the relationship necessary for sharing faith. The acronym, "for sinners" is a helpful and simple tool which helps evangelizers recognize basic human issues encountered in the process of establishing rapport and identifying with others. This acronym implies mutuality of the participants, in that evangelization is accomplished by sinners for sinners. Each letter of the phrase reminds us of conversation starters which enable us to go beyond the weather or the local baseball team in our initial conversations. Using this acronym is an excellent means to develop communication skill in any social circumstance, by the way.

F—Family
O—Occupation
R—Recreation

S—Setting, Situation
I—Interests
N—Natural Abilities
N—Needs
E—Expectations
R—Response
S—Spiritual Survey

We do not use this tool in order to gather information, as for a census, but we use it as an aid in establishing rapport and inviting the other person into a trusting relationship. We would never use this acronym as an interviewing tool, for instance; instead, it is offered as a helpful means of engaging the other person in worth-while conversation.

Faith-Sharing

Often, when we are presenting our training seminars, the trainees initially think that they have no faith stories to share. This is probably because, as Catholics, we have not been taught to think in terms of sharing our experiences of God with others. For many of us, faith has always been one-dimensional, private, and personal.

However, sharing our own faith stories quite often reminds the participants of their own faith stories. "Gee, that reminds me of a time when God . . ." And this is one of the primary purposes of faith sharing: to elicit the faith stories of other people. Faith sharing strengthens our own faith and the faith of others as we tell our stories and we hear others tell theirs.

We ask our trainees to describe times when God has touched their lives significantly and to tell how their lives were changed through these experiences. These stories can be dramatic Paul-being-knocked-to-the-ground stories or the more ordinary Elijah-finding-God-not-in-the-earthquake-or-in-the-hurricane-but-in-the-gentle-whisper-of-the-wind stories.

As their training continues, our trainees realize that, like all of us, they have many faith stories, many times in their lives when they have experienced God one way or another. It is this rich reservoir of stories that they will share with the people whom they visit. There are several guidelines which we ask our trainees to remember as they retell their stories of faith: no travelogues, brevity, giving glory to God, no stories of a confessional nature.

The spirit of mutuality prevails during this step of the process, too. It is important for us to remember that we, as visitors, are not the only ones with faith stories to share. We encourage those whom we are visiting to share their faith experiences with us, also. Most of the time, they don't even have to be asked, for their faith-sharing arises as a natural result of hearing the stories which we share with them. Our self disclosures give the people we visit permission to share their own faith stories. We have found that people love to talk about their faith, given a chance. Many people will tell us that they yearn to talk about their faith with others but usually do not have an opportunity.

There are both positive and negative faith stories, and quite often, we will hear negative stories from the people we visit. These negative stories usually reflect the person's anger, frustration, or lack of faith. I remember one man who said to me, "All this faith stuff may be fine for you, but let me tell you how angry I am with the Catholic church!" His story included the fact that a priest would not anoint his dying mother because she was not a member of his parish. "The last time I set foot in a Catholic church was twenty years ago at my mother's funeral!"

What do we do when we hear these negative stories which range from anger at a priest, frustration with the hypocrisy of the laity, to, frequently, anger at God? We advise our trainees always to respect the sacredness of the story. I listened carefully to this man's story and respected the fact that this was his experience. Then, we advise our trainees to acknowledge the negative emotion and help the person to vent it. "You really are angry, aren't you?", I responded. He then went on for another ten minutes about how angry he was. The worst thing we could have done at this stage would have been to say, "Oh, you really shouldn't feel that way!" This would only discount the validity of his experience and alienate him further.

The next step is to ask the people if, in their anger or absence, they have missed anything. Before I knew it, this man said, "Well, yes, I really miss the Eucharist most of all. It's been so long, and I also miss my quiet visits to the church. I used to make visits when the church was empty, and it was so peaceful there . . ."

The final step—after respecting their stories, helping them to acknowledge and vent their emotions, and inviting them to remember positive aspects of their faith—is to invite them to allow their faith to transcend the negative experience. Finally, I asked him, "Do you think that there is any way that you could possibly get beyond your anger and allow your faith to transcend it so you can get on with your life?" In this case, his response was positive, and I was able to begin the third step of our process, sharing "the Christ story" with him. To do that, we use a transitional question such as, "Now that we've discussed our faith experiences with each other, can we see what the Bible says about our faith?"

The Christ Story

Most Catholics find it difficult if not impossible to proclaim the Gospel message simply because we have never been trained to present it nor were we ever expected to present it. During our seminars, our trainees are prepared to present the four central truths of the Gospel simply, accurately, effectively, confidently, and joyfully.

In theological terms, the four central truths are creation, the fall, incarnation, and redemption. However, we translate this terminology into simple over-the-coffee-cup language when we present these truths. They become:

> Creation . . . . .God's Plan
> The Fall . . . . .Our Problem
> Incarnation . . . . .God's Solution
> Redemption . . . . .Our Response

It is impossible here to include all of the material in the training manual which deals with the Christ story, but by the time our trainees have finished these sessions, they are amazed at the ease with which they can present the gospel message and support it scripturally.

Invitation to Conversion

The fourth step in the evangelization process is to invite people into an on-going, deeper conversion. I often tell our trainees that if I were visiting Mother Teresa herself or Pope John Paul II, I wouldn't hesitate to invite them to conversion also. None of us has arrived, and we are all continuing on our journeys of faith.

It is this awareness of the constant need for conversion in our own lives that allows us to invite others into conversion. Conversion is a process for us; it is not an event as some Protestants view it. We see conversion as a continual process, a process which began even before we were born. Some evangelical or pentecostal evangelists would view conversion as a specific event, occurring at a specific time and place in their history. How often have we heard our evangelical brothers and sisters say, "Well, I was saved at a Billy Graham rally on June 4, 1973, at four o'clock in the afternoon." As Catholics, we believe that we were saved two thousand years ago, and when asked if we have been "born again," our response is, "Yes, I have been born again and again and again and again . . . ."

After befriending people, sharing our faith stories, and proclaiming the gospel message, the next step is to invite them into deeper conversion. We ask the questions, "Has Christ come alive in your life? Would you like to have a deeper, stronger, more personal relationship with him than you ever have had before? Would you like us to pray with you now, asking him to come into all of our lives in a new way?" Most people can't resist this invitation, but I always give them options by suggesting that perhaps they would like to pray privately or that maybe the timing isn't right and they would prefer waiting.

If their response is positive, we pray with them right then and there using printed prayer cards which we carry with us. I find that most people are more comfortable if I explain exactly how we will pray together so that there are no surprises. I explain that first I will lead an opening prayer, next we will read the prayer card together, and then I will close with prayer. This may sound simplistic, but we have found that people are much more comfortable when they know exactly what is expected of them. This is especially true for people who are not familiar with spontaneous prayer.

Integration into Community

The final step is to assist them to be integrated into a faith community and help them to live a balanced Christian life. The five necessary components of a balanced Christian life include prayer, worship, Scripture, witness, and service. We carry with us specific literature—to give to the people during this step of the process—which deals with each of these components including a parish bulletin, ministries directory, Gospel of John, a tract on prayer, and a pamphlet which reinforces our presentation of the Gospel message.

Integration into a community of worshipers is essential, particularly if we are to avoid the Jesus-and-me syndrome of "Who needs church?" The action taken during this step will vary depending upon the needs of the people, but our goal here is to *introduce* or *re-introduce* them into a vibrant, alive faith community. If they are not members of our parish, then perhaps we introduce them to the coordinator of the parish Rite of Christian Initiation of Adults program. If they are separated or divorced, we could introduce them to the chairperson of the parish or diocesan singles ministry. Prayer groups or Bible study groups are other good introductory resources for these people; it all depends on their particular needs. If they are in need of confession, we might ask them if they would like to meet with the pastor or his associate.

Whatever their needs are, our role should be one of introduction only. This is how we define the limitations of the role of evangelizer: we do not need to become the person's personal pastor or teacher. It is time now—after we have evangelized them through witness, proclamation and invitation—to hand them over to the pastors and teachers in our community. The ministry of friendship never ends, but we do not need to feel responsible for these people for the rest of their lives.

This basically is the content of the training course *Mission: Evangelization.* These local seminars, of varying lengths, are usually offered by clusters of parishes, by diocesan offices, or, occasionally, by universities or seminaries. A video-taped introduction to the *Mission: Evangelization* course is also included as part of the follow-up programs for the Isaiah 43 Parish Missions; then, the entire course is facilitated on the parish level by lay facilitators.

To date, we have trained thousands of Catholic evangelizers in more than one hundred parishes in approximately twenty states and in several Canadian provinces, and the good news about this method is that it works!

Notes

1. Blum, Deshaies, Stokloza, op. cit.

9

Hospitality—A Vital Evangelistic Ministry

The ministry of hospitality is vital to long-term effective evangelization. As evangelizers, we must ask ourselves, "Into what are we welcoming these newcomers?" If our parishes are not vibrant and alive, we wonder if we are not setting live chicks under dead hens.

Hospitality is a ministry which must pervade all aspects of parish ministry—liturgy, catechesis, support groups, adult education groups, and prayer groups. The parish secretary must be hospitable; the groundskeeper must be a welcoming person; the rectory housekeeper can affect the tone of a whole parish. Every single person from the youngest child enrolled in a CCD class to the oldest pillar-of-the-church parishioner must be hospitable and welcoming if evangelization is to succeed in that parish. And the spirit of hospitality must be genuine if strangers are truly to feel welcome.

Institutional Hospitality

Sometimes, a parish can do all the "right" things, yet its efforts at hospitality can come off as insincere. Let me give you an example of what I have come to call institutional hospitality, in which all of the "right" things are done, but somehow people don't feel welcome.

A few years ago, I attended a national convention of Catholic professionals for the first-timer. As a newcomer, I was given an identification badge with a yellow ribbon identifying me as a "first timer"; I was invited to a newcomer's luncheon; and later that first evening, a newcomer's reception. My name was even printed in the program as a "first-timer." I was very impressed at the lengths to which the group's administrative board had gone to make me feel welcome.

What I actually experienced was another matter. Although the organization had done many of the "right" things, including introducing newcomers to the established members, we found many cliques among them where we were really not welcome at all. I made many conscious attempts to meet older members but met mostly with indifference. At the newcomer's reception, I actually found myself attempting to join conversations, attempting to introduce myself to many of these older members, and yet finding a coldness whose reasons eluded me. This was not my normal experience as a newcomer even at secular events. In fact, at secular events, I found myself far more welcome and included than I did at this particular convention.

In the South, we would call this organization "a good ole boys' club," neither desiring nor welcoming newcomers to join them. As a result, I left the convention two days early, never to return to active membership in this group. While the organization actually did many of the "right" things to make me feel welcome, I never *felt* welcome, and that made all the difference in the world.

Sometimes, our parishes do all the "right" things to make newcomers feel welcome, but if a genuine spirit of hospitality is not present among its members, the newcomers will not feel welcome and will leave, searching for a sense of belonging elsewhere. Parishes may offer greeters at the door and coffee and donuts after the Mass, but if the parishioners themselves do not offer an authentic spirit of welcome, these efforts at hospitality will fail.

The ministry of hospitality plays an especially important role when we consider the size of our Catholic parishes. The average Protestant congregation has two hundred men, women, and children. The average Catholic parish numbers over 2,500 parishioners. My own parish has 3,100 families enrolled, a total of more than ten thousand people! How difficult it is to establish a sense of community in these large parishes, yet just because of their size, how much more important hospitality becomes!

I recall reading that a survey of hospitality in many Protestant churches found that none of them scored more than minimally on the questionnaires. I have oftened wondered what would happen if a similar survey would be designed for Catholic parishes.

As a result of my curiosity, I have designed the following survey for you. Please visit Catholic parishes, rate them in terms of hospitality, and return the results to me for tabulation and evaluation.

Hospitality Survey

Please visit a Catholic parish and allocate ten points for each positive response to the following statements:

_____ 1. I was welcomed at the door to the church or in the gathering space of the church.
_____ 2. I was welcomed through word or eye contact by the person next to me as I entered the pew.
_____ 3. The priest or lector welcomed newcomers during their introductory comments.
_____ 4. Newcomers were recognized and identified during the course of the Mass.
_____ 5. Newcomers were personally greeted by other parishioners during the course of the Mass.
_____ 6. At the Sign of Peace, I felt sincerely welcomed or greeted by people near me.

_____ 7. After Mass, there was an opportunity for me to meet other people—coffee and donuts or whatever.

_____ 8. During this time, I was welcomed and greeted by at least one parishioner.

_____ 9. During this time, I was included in interesting conversation.

_____10. During this time, I was introduced to at least one other parishioner.

_____11. I was invited to come back.

_____12. I was invited to come to parish activities other than Mass.

_____13. I was introduced to the pastor, an associate pastor, or another staff person.

_____14. I felt truly welcomed and would look forward to attending this church again.

Total score:_____

Name of
Parish _____

Address _____

City_____ State _____Zip _____

This survey only addresses the issue of hospitality at a Sunday liturgy and, from this point of view, is incomplete. However, the survey might be helpful just in encouraging parishes to reassess and reevaluate their efforts at hospitality.

It is not impossible for a Catholic parish to score a perfect 140 points on this survey. I attended Mass at a church near where I live in South Florida which exhibited all of these qualities. I was greeted initially in the parking lot by a parishioner who simply said, "Hi! I don't know if I know you. Is this the first time you've come to our church?" Then, newcomers were welcomed by the priest at the beginning of Mass and later identified during the Mass in a very non-threatening way. Right after the Prayers of the Faithful, the pastor simply asked all of us who were attending this church for the first time to remain standing for a few minutes. Everyone else sat down, and then he thanked us for coming and publicly welcomed us.

Meanwhile, those parishioners surrounding us apparently took notice of who the newcomers were. During the Sign of Peace, I was not only welcomed but I was handed a small pamphlet entitled, "Welcome to Our Parish," which included vital information concerning the schedule of Masses and Confession and a listing of support groups or adult education programs which were available. At the conclusion of the Mass, I was invited for coffee and donuts; during that time I was introduced to several members of the parish, including the pastor. I really felt welcome and have returned many times to this particular church. I would join this parish if it were not for the fact that I already belong to a dynamic, alive parish.

Hospitality is vitally important in every phase of parish life, not just at Sunday Mass. One of the most important areas is that of religious instruction. Our teachers, our principals, our CCD instructors must be trained in evangelization skills, for they have daily opportunities to evangelize both students and parents. Our parish secretaries are quite often the first contact that newcomers have with the parish. Our parish housekeepers, welcoming visitors to the rectory, should be trained in techniques of hospitality. All of us, as members of our parishes, should be aware of welcoming strangers—and not just with a perfunctory handshake at the time of the Sign of Peace.

In a parish to which I formerly belonged in Albany, New York, a group of parishioners stumbled upon a wonderful way of welcoming strangers, making new friends, and forming community. Several of us decided that we would initiate an informal come-home-for-breakfast program in our parish, unbeknown to the pastor or anyone else. We decided that on a given Sunday each month, we would look around us at Mass and find a family whom we didn't know. Then, after Mass, we would invite them home to have a simple breakfast of coffee, juice and donuts with us.

The families involved in this little project sought out families similar to their own, with children close to the ages of their own children. Although our guests usually were surprised at our invitations, there were no refusals. After we visited for a while in our homes, we told them that there was only one request that we made of them: that they, too, on the third Sunday of the month would join us and invite a family home with them. Eventually, our little band of "breakfasteers" grew and there was quite a network of hospitality going on in that parish.

It was simple, informal, with no budget. Yet asking strangers to breakfast became a way of making new friends and of inviting them into involvement in parish activities. Our pastor didn't know about this project until nearly a year had passed.

The ways of offering hospitality are limited only by our creativity and imagination. But one thing is certain: if our efforts at hospitality are insincere, they will be ineffective. Like children, newcomers can spot a phony a mile away!

10

The Challenge of Evangelization

The ministry of evangelization is challenging. Jesus' first and last recorded words challenge us today: "Come, and I will make you fishers of men," and "Go, ye, therefore into the whole world and make disciples . . . ." Between the "coming" and the "going," there is a world of challenge!

This dual challenge of invitation and sending forth are echoed in Joseph Cardinal Bernardin's twofold definition of evangelization. He describes evangelization as involving "two simultaneous processes: the ongoing evangelization and conversion of ourselves as a Church and the movement into the world to share the Good News."[1]

As we actually become the Good News, it is essential to share that Good News with others. Basically, this involves two processes—our own conversion and then sharing ourselves with others. As evangelizers, we are constantly being called to conversion—that gentle growth, that transformation into Christ, that unfinished business of change in our lives. As that transformation continues, we are called to share our new life with others.

Neither process is easy! Change hurts, and it is often much easier to resist any change in our attitudes, our thoughts, our hearts. Even the suggestion that we may need to change some of our attitudes may be insulting! Conversion means change— not change for the sake of change but a "turning around" of previously held principles, beliefs, or behaviors because of new insights and understanding.

Conversion means growth. A continual process in our lives, conversion ever deepens, ever widens our spiritual, physical, emotional, and mental lives. And conversion, I believe, is developmental and hierarchical. Just as a little child must be able to walk before it can run, we also must be ready for conversion—physically, mentally, emotionally, and spiritually ready to take the next step in our sanctification, which I describe as becoming all that God intended for us to be in the first place when we were created.

To become all that God intended us to be requires openness and a willingness to grow, to change. Sadly, many people are so fearful of change that they become stagnant. Unfortunately, the longer they remain at a static level, the less likely they will be able to change. As a result, we see many Christians who have never really seen and tasted the goodness of the Lord to the full extent possible. They are good people, beautiful people, but sadly undersanctified, for lack of a better word. They lead dull lives; they are satisfied with the status quo; and they view change of any kind as threatening.

Fortunately, most people do not remain stagnant. The psychologist, Dr. Thomas Harris, tells us that people will change when (1) they hurt enough, (2) they are bored enough, or (3) they believe they can change.

This secular theory of change, of course, is only one theory in the growing field of psychology and does not allow for the supernatural element, the gentle—and sometimes not so gentle—action of the Spirit. However, it corroborates the need for readiness for change in a person's life. A person who is absolutely content will not change and will not seek growth, for growth may upset contentedness.

"Create a crisis!"

It has been said that Jesus came to comfort the disturbed and disturb the comfortable. As evangelizers, are we not called to do the same? Jesus was a rabble rouser, inciting riots constantly. Are we not also called to be rabble-rousers?

By ourselves, we are never going to convert anyone; we simply do not have the power to convert people. But as evangelizers, we are called to be facilitators of conversion, facilitators of change. How do we do this? How do we facilitate conversion? I suggest that we *do* become rabble-rousers, presenting others with the evidence of our transformed lives, sharing the reason for that transformation, and inviting them into a revolutionary way of living and dying. As evangelizers, we need to "disturb the comfortable" and, in their new discomfort, offer them comfort and growth through relationship with Jesus and integration into his community of disciples.

In the early days of my involvement with Catholic evangelization, I used to get so frustrated co-ordinating the parish evangelization council. I would ask my pastor, "How can we evangelize when most of our parishioners don't want to be evangelized? They don't want to grow; they don't want to change." His answer, which I thought was flippant at the time, was, "Create a crisis!" Over the years, I have come to realize the wisdom in that advice.

As evangelizers, we do have the power to "create a crisis" in the lives of those around us. We are not talking about creating tragedies in their lives; we are talking about the possibility of creating disharmony, dissonance, doubt. People cannot live with dissonance for very long. They must resolve the disharmony in their lives and either return to their former way of thinking and believing, often with more determination and confidence, or move onto a new level of faith and understanding—usually with a great deal of fear and trepidation as they face the unknown.

"Crisis" in My Own Life

Several years ago, when I was editing *The Catholic Evangelist* magazine, I had repeatedly been invited to visit Haiti with Ferdinand Mahfood, founder and director of Food for the Poor, a ministry to the indigent in the Caribbean. It was not until Archbishop McCarthy intervened and personally asked me to go that I agreed. However, I decided that my story on the poor in Haiti and on the ministry of Food for the Poor was going to be unemotional; I would maintain professional journalistic standards of objectivity and detachment and get the facts, just the facts.

My objectivity flew out the window after I had been in Haiti about ten minutes. I saw poverty which was beyond my belief! Haiti is the poorest country in the Western hemisphere, and I saw people living like animals—no, worse than our animals. Ten to twelve people lived in tiny little shacks no larger than our bathrooms. These shacks lined alleyways with open trenches of raw sewage flowing through them. I watched Haitian mothers bathe their children in this sewage water, the only water available to them.

Haitians eat only once every three days if they're lucky. No wonder half of their babies die before the age of five! As a mother of four healthy children, I really had to look at that statistic: which fifty percent of my children would I have been willing to sacrifice if I had been raising my children in these inhuman, deplorable conditions?

Talk about a crisis! Talk about cognitive dissonance! During that trip to Haiti, I had to come to grips with my own attitudes toward the poor, and while I was ashamed to admit it, I realized that up until then, I really hadn't cared that much about the poor. I had written perfunctory articles concerning the poor migrant farmers west of us in Florida. We had always contributed to the Thanksgiving canned goods drive and the Christmas clothing drive in our parish. But, ashamed, I had to admit that deep down I really wasn't at all concerned about the poor.

My trip to Haiti disturbed me and shook me out of my complacency. I began to see the face of Jesus in the poor. I experienced profound conversion, and my life has never been the same since.

I came back and wrote an article entitled, "An Enraged Mother's Tears" and have been begging for the poor unashamedly at every opportunity. Convinced of the efficacy of Food for the Poor, I have joined their staff full-time. I have written many articles since then on behalf of the poor, and through my contacts with the Catholic Press Association, I have helped to arrange for more than a hundred other writers or editors from diocesan or national publications to experience similar pilgrimages to Haiti.

Archbishop McCarthy and Ferdinand Mahfood were facilitators of conversion for me. Rabble-rousers, they created a crisis in my life, a time of disharmony and dissonance. My old comfortable attitudes about the poor were no longer acceptable to me; I had a choice to make, and I chose to change those attitudes. My faith grew; another dimension of faith was introduced and integrated. I now experience God's love in and through the poor; I am united with them, not out of a sense of guilt, but in a spirit of solidarity and compassion. I thank God for the rabble-rousers in my life who, through their own witness, their own countercultural life styles, their own transformed lives, jolt me out of my comfortableness and invite me to conversion.

Mother Teresa is a rabble-rouser. Dorothy Day was a rabble-rouser. Martin Luther King, Jr. was a rabble-rouser. My friend, Ferdinand Mahfood, who founded Food for the Poor six years ago and adopted nine million poor people in the Caribbean is a rabble-rouser. Billie, the mother of the AIDS patient, is a rabble-rouser. The bishops, priests, religious and laypeople who live out their faith are rabble-rousers.

THE CHALLENGE OF EVANGELIZATION

As contemporary evangelizers, we are on the cutting edge of a new millennium of Christianity. We can make a difference now and in the future.

"One does the best that one can"

There is a story about a crazy little bird, a sparrow, who in the midst of nuclear holocaust sings, soars, and performs all kinds of wondrous feats in the air. Then he lies down and points his two spindly little legs toward the sky as if to ward off the horrible, impending disaster. When questioned, he replies, "One does the best that one can!"

The little bird reminds me of people I know, all "blind beggars" who are doing the best they can. Being ourselves and being the best we can be is our greatest asset as evangelizers. We do not need to be public figures or professional evangelists; we do not need to be theologians or Scripture scholars. We need to be trained, formed, and informed as committed, articulate evangelizers, but we will rely on our own faith, integrity, zeal, and experience as we go out into the world to evangelize.

Realizing that we are called, gifted, commanded, and empowered to share our faith, we will go forth sowing in tears but reaping in joy. There is no question whether there is a harvest or even whether it is ripe—the question is, "Who will be God's instruments?"

Recently, a laywoman shared with us an analogy, comparing us with reeds growing in a marsh. At some point God looks down upon all of these beautiful reeds, swaying in the wind, and uproots us. God holds us gently, considering all of the possibilities. Then, we are hollowed out, completely emptied, and punched full of holes. Only then are we ready to receive the divine breath of life, and from that energizing, life-giving breath comes beautiful music. We become God's instruments, yielding haunting melodies. We sing God's song, and it is a love song.

Are we evangelizers willing to be chosen, emptied, formed as his instruments? Are we willing to acknowledge that we are called and gifted? Are we willing to be the hands, the feet, the voice, the Body, broken and shared?

Notes

1. Joseph Cardinal Bernardin, *Catholic Evangelization Today* (New York: Paulist Press, 1987), p. 1.

Evangelization Resources

National Council of Catholic Evangelization
P.O. Box 10525
Chicago, Illinois 60610-0525 (312) 280-1029

Paulist National Catholic Evangelization Association
3031 Fourth Street, N.E.
Washington, D.C. 20017 (202) 832-5022

These two national organizations both provide excellent resource material for evangelization. However, be sure to ask the Paulists for their *Pentecost '88 Resource Directory*, a comprehensive resource guide of national, diocesan, and parish evangelization resources.